BEARCUB BIOS

SUPREME COURT JUSTICE

by Spencer Brinker

Consultant: Beth Gambro
Reading Specialist, Yorkville, Illinois

Minneapolis, Minnesota

Teaching Tips

BEFORE READING
- Discuss what a biography is. What kinds of things might a biography tell a reader?
- Look through the glossary together. Read and discuss the words.
- Go on a picture walk, looking through the pictures to discuss vocabulary and make predictions about the text.

DURING READING
- Encourage readers to point to each word as it is read. Stop occasionally to ask readers to point to a specific word in the text.
- If a reader encounters an unknown word, ask them to look at the rest of the page. Are there any clues to help them understand?

AFTER READING
- Check for understanding.
    - Where was Sonia Sotomayor born?
    - What does she do?
    - What does she care about?
- Ask the readers to think deeper.
    - If you met Sonia, what question would you like to ask her? Why?

Credits:
Cover and title page, © Supreme Court of the United States/Public Domain and © stock_photo_world/Shutterstock; 3, © KAREN BLEIER/Getty Images; 5, © PAUL J. RICHARDS/Getty Images; 7, © WhiteHouse.gov/CC 3.0 Attribution License; 8, © WhiteHouse.gov/CC 3.0 Attribution License; 11, © WhiteHouse.gov/CC 3.0 Attribution License; 12-13, © everything possible/Shutterstock; 15, © John Iacono/Getty Images; 16-17, © George Napolitano/Getty Images; 18-19, © JEWEL SAMAD/Getty Images; 21, © Brooks Kraft/Getty Images; 22, © K2 images/Shutterstock; 23TL, © IPGGutenbergUKLtd/iStock; 23TC, © Alex Wong/Getty Images; 23TR, © simpson33/iStock; 23BL, © Flamingo Images/Shutterstock; and 23BR, © Ogphoto/iStock.

Library of Congress Cataloging-in-Publication Data

Names: Brinker, Spencer– author. Title: Sonia Sotomayor : Supreme Court justice / Spencer Brinker. Description: New York, NY : Bearport Publishing Company, 2020. | Series: Bearcub bios | Includes bibliographical references and index. Identifiers: LCCN 2020000517 (print) | LCCN 2020000518 (ebook) | ISBN 9781642809831 (library binding) | ISBN 9781642809947 (paperback) | ISBN 9781647470050 (ebook) Subjects: LCSH: Sotomayor, Sonia, 1954–Juvenile literature. | Judges—United States—Biography—Juvenile literature. | United States. Supreme Court—Officials and employees—Biography—Juvenile literature. Classification: LCC KF8745.S67 R67 2020 (print) | LCC KF8745.S67 (ebook) | DDC 347.73/2634 [B]—dc23
LC record available at https://lccn.loc.gov/2020000517LC ebook record available at https://lccn.loc.gov/2020000518

Copyright © 2021 Bearport Publishing Company. All rights reserved. No part of this publication may be reproduced in whole or in part, stored in any retrieval system, or transmitted in any form or by any means, electronic, mechanical, photocopying, recording, or otherwise, without written permission from the publisher.

For more information, write to Bearport Publishing, 5357 Penn Avenue South, Minneapolis, MN 55419.

Printed in the United States of America.

Contents

On the Supreme Court 4

Sonia's Life 6

Did You Know?........................... 22

Glossary 23

Index 24

Read More 24

Learn More Online....................... 24

About the Author 24

On the Supreme Court

Sonia Sotomayor hugged her mother.

She smiled at her brother.

Sonia just became a **justice** on the **Supreme Court**!

She would be a top judge.

Sonia's Life

Sonia was born in New York.

Her parents came from an island called Puerto Rico.

Her family spoke Spanish at home.

When she was little, she saw a TV show with a court.

This made her want to be a **lawyer**!

Sonia did well in school.

Sonia became a lawyer.

She worked hard at her job.

She cared about being fair.

Then, Sonia became a judge.

She said what was right.

She learned about many problems.

One time, baseball players said the team owners were not fair.

They needed help to solve the problem.

Sonia agreed with the players.

She made the owners be fair.

The baseball games started again!

In 2009, Barack Obama was president.

He needed a new judge for the Supreme Court.

He picked Sonia.

Sonia was the third woman ever on the Supreme Court.

She was the first **Hispanic** justice.

Sonia's hard work paid off!

Did You Know?

Born: June 25, 1954

Family: Celina (mother), Juan (father), Juan (brother)

When she was a kid: When Sonia was seven years old, doctors told her she had **diabetes**.

Special fact: Sonia Sotomayor loves the Yankees baseball team.

Sonia says: "I always look at the positive."

Life Connections

Sonia works hard for what she cares about. What things do you care about? How do you work hard for those things?

Glossary

diabetes a sickness where there is too much sugar in the blood

Hispanic a person who comes from a place where Spanish is spoken

justice a judge on the Supreme Court

lawyer a person who helps people with law problems

Supreme Court the highest court in the United States

Index

baseball 14, 16, 22
judge 4, 12, 19
justice 4, 20
lawyer 9–10
New York 6
Supreme Court 4, 19–20

Read More

Kortuem, Amy. *The U.S. Supreme Court (U.S. Government)*. North Mankato, MN: Pebble (2020).

Polinsky, Paige V. *Sonia Sotomayor: Supreme Court Justice (Blastoff! Readers: Women Leading the Way)*. Minneapolis: Bellwether Media (2019).

Learn More Online

1. Go to **www.factsurfer.com**
2. Enter "**Sonia Sotomayor**" into the search box.
3. Click on the cover of this book to see a list of websites.

About the Author

Spencer Brinker loves to tell "dad jokes" and play word games with his twin girls.